## PART 1

SCOUTING:
Prepare To Win!

by Joe Bertuzzi

This book was written to help coaches learn how to effectively scout a future opponent and evaluate and assess the information. The text teaches you how to prepare your team for team meetings and scout team training sessions. Also, you are walked through your pregame speech, pregame warm-up, and how to make adjustments during the first half of the match.

Published by
REEDSWAIN INC

Table of Contents - Part One

Introduction - Scouting - Prepare to Win! iii

How to Scout and How to Use This Guide iv

Pregame and Organization iv-1

Goalkeeper Pregame Assessment 1

Team System of Play 1

Individual Player Assessments 1-3

The Attack - Tactics 3

The Attack - Corner Kicks 3-4

The Attack - Free Kicks 4

The Attack - Throw-ins, Goal Kicks, Kickoffs 4-5

The Attack - Scoring Opportunities 5

Penalty Kicks - Shooter and Keeper .5-6

The Defense - Tactics 6

The Defense - Corner Kicks 8

The Defense - Free Kicks 8

The Defense - Kick-offs 8

Preparing for a Team Meeting and
Scout Team Training Sessions 9-11

Game Day - Pregame Locker Room .10

Game Day - Pregame Warm-up 10

The Match 10-11

Table of Contents - Part Two

Page Thumb Index

Pregame Organization . . . . .13 . . . .**PG**

Goalkeeper Pregame Assessment . . . . .14 . . . .**GK**

Team System of Play . . . . .15 . . .**SP**

Individual Player Assessments . . . . .16-19 .**PA**

Key To Diagrams . . . . .20 . . . .**K**

The Attack . . . . .21 . . . .**A**

The Attack - Tactics . . . . .22 . . . .**AT**

The Attack - Corner Kicks . . . . .23 . . . .**AC**

The Attack - Free Kicks . . . . .24 . . . .**AF**

The Attack . . . . .25 . . . .**AT**
  Throw-ins
  Goal Kicks
  Kick Offs

The Attack - Scoring Opportunities . . . . .26 . . . .**SO**

Penalty Kicks . . . . .27 . . . .**PK**

The Defense . . . . .28 . . . .**D**

The Defense - Tactics . . . . .29 . . . .**DT**

The Defense . . . . .30 . . . .**DC**
  Corner Kicks
  Free Kicks
  Penalty Kicks
  Kick Off

Team Meeting Prep Sheet . . . . .31 . . . .**TM**

INTRODUCTION

SCOUTING - PREPARE TO WIN!

Your preparation and assessment of what you see and how you analyze this information will have a direct impact on all of your matches. How you prepare your team prior to kickoff and how you determine what adjustments should be made dictates the direction your team will follow. The Soccer Scouting Guide is written to help you prepare your team for an upcoming opponent.

There are page numbers on the bottom of the scout guide. Use them in conjunction with the text. This will enable you to better understand the concepts on how to scout. You will be able to flip back and forth to the corresponding text and guide. After you have developed a foundation on scouting assessment then use only the *unique thumb index* which allows you to quickly move from section to section as the flow of the game continues. Through repetition, you will find that the ease of the thumb guide enables you to evaluate the various parameters of the game more efficiently.

As you work through the text on the following pages in regard to how to scout and the importance of each section of the guide you will instantly take on a new understanding and respect for your opponent.

I personally walk you through all facets of scouting on a page by page basis. I will discuss how to neutralize an opponent's strengths and how to attack their weaknesses. Through the use of this guide you will become a better prepared coach who will then be able to lead your team toward success.

DEDICATION

I dedicate this scouting guide to my parents who have prepared me well for life.

A special thank you to Chris Masullo and Kristen Benevenga. Their computer graphics skill has enabled me to develop this scout guide.

How To Scout and How To Use This Guide
Preparation = Success

If you were to ask one of my best friends and colleagues of the game Coach Jack Weber what is my greatest contribution to the game he would probably reply, 'His preparation - of food.' Coach Weber and I have scouted many games together. My backpack is always filled with my scouting guides, clipboards, homemade soup, tea and lemon, and Cheez-its. Wherever we travel together to scout a match we share our perceptions of the game and, of course, my food.

I will discuss each page of the scouting guide in detail. Once you have read the text it would be beneficial to you to scout a preseason opponent. After you have evaluated and analyzed your opponent you can teach your team through a team meeting and team training session how to attack and defend your opponents' strengths and weaknesses. This will impress upon your team the importance of preparation and how to collectively execute a strategical game plan as one unit. The clarity from your perspective as to how to do this will become evident as you follow my step by step approach through the scouting guide.

In many sections of this guide there will be 'Questions To Be Answered.' These are questions which must be addressed by you during your scouting, evaluation, and analysis. Re-read the 'Questions To Be Answered' just prior to scouting the match so they will be fresh in your mind. There will be specific pages (15, 16, 21 and 28) that will be completed after the match. This will help in preparing the Team Meeting Prep Sheet.

It is a great idea to scout with an assistant. Four eyes are definitely better than two. You can then break up the guide into attack and defense, each of you scouting a topic. The difficult time approaches during tournaments when you play the winner of the match you are watching. In this situation the primary scout will watch the team you think will win. As the game unfolds, if it does not go the way you predicted, switch guides so the primary scout is watching your next opponent.

To any coach who says 'I do not have the time to scout,' my simple answer is "Preparation is part of the game. Find a way to scout and you have **FOUND A WAY TO WIN!**"

PREGAME AND ORGANIZATION, THUMB INDEX • PG - Page 13.
Early arrival before pregame warm-up allows you to set-up and organize before kickoff. Equally as important, you can begin to evaluate the technical abilities of individual players during this time. This will be discussed in detail on pages 1 through 3.

Determining the field size of the match you are seeing and relating it to the size of the field you will play your opponent on is important. Technical teams like to use space (large fields) whereas a weaker opponent becomes stronger defensively if they are on a small field and can find a way to deny time and space. Weather conditions many times dictate how much energy a team expends. Extremes in heat, cold, and rain can influence the outcome of a match. The halftime score is relative to the game you are seeing. Ultimately, it would be great to see your opponent play an equal or better team. Many times because of your training and game schedule you are limited to which game you can see. We have all witnessed matches that were over in the first ten minutes. If this is the case, then concentrate on a team's set pieces and individual techniques. Team tactics and adjustments are difficult to assess in a blow-out game. Many substitutes play in this type of match. Evaluate both their technical abilities and how they conform to team tactics. You can still get some concept of how a team is organized (system of play) and how they play within the system. If the match you are witnessing is a great one pay close attention to team tactics. This will be vital to your team's success. Scouting tactics are addressed later in this guide.

GOALKEEPER PREGAME ASSESSMENT, THUMB INDEX • GK - Page 14.

It is important to assess a goalkeeper prior to the kickoff. This is because if he is not challenged during a match, you can analyze some of his strengths and weaknesses. This time allows you to assess his technical abilities. As the keeper goes through his warm-up note on the pregame assessment form next to the respective titles all the pros and cons of his technical game. During the match you continue with a technical/tactical assessment of the keeper using the individual player assessment form found on page 17.

TEAM SYSTEM OF PLAY, THUMB INDEX • SP - Page 15.

As the team is lining-up for the kickoff and as soon as the match begins, write down the uniform numbers of the players in their respective positions on the full field diagram. You can quickly see what system of play they are using. (This will also help with the individual player assessments). Understanding their system of play and where specific players are placed within this system will aid you in attacking their system.

INDIVIDUAL PLAYER ASSESSMENTS, THUMB INDEX • PA - Pages 16-19.

In this section you will use phrases or single words to describe a player's technical ability and role within the teams' system. Include any weaknesses seen and how to attack them. Record the size of each player. Also, any cards given should be written. If a player was given a card due to his temper please note this.

I will now describe how to be more specific in regard to the individual player being assessed. First, let us start with the **goalkeeper**. Pregame you began to assess his technical ability. Continue with this evaluation.

Questions To Be Answered:
- How does he direct the defense?
- What is his positioning on all dead ball situations?
- Where is his starting position and when does he retreat during the flow of the match?
- How does he control his box?
- How does he start the attack?
  Style of play many times dictates this.
- Pregame you may have observed him handling crosses well but now you can

assess how he performs this task in a crowd.

- Is the goalkeeper composed?
- How is his composure affected after a goal is given up?
- If there was a penalty kick - what was his reaction and decision?

This should be listed on the penalty kick page of this guide (page 27).

Next, let us discuss how to arrange the field players on the individual player assessment form. The boxes directly below the goalkeeper box are used for defenders. How many boxes used is directly related to the number of defenders your opponent uses. If they use a traditional four back marking system, reserve the first box for the sweeper, the second one for the stopper. The next two boxes are for the outside defenders. If a flat back system is used reserve the first box for the first central defender. With flat back systems of four the next box is used for the second central defender. After all the defenders are listed, the next box is for a defensive central midfielder. List the flank midfielders, followed by the attacking midfielders, and last, the strikers/front runners. The reason I have spent so much time discussing the order in which the field players are placed on the form is because by linking the players together you can rapidly flip back to this section and instantly jot a quick comment in the appropriate box. Continuity allows you to work more efficiently.

Assess the **defenders**' technical and tactical ability and level of fitness.

Questions To Be Answered:
- Identify the weak foot - we always force the ball onto it.

- You must identify the weak link defender. If this is a team that builds out of the back we want him with the ball and on his weak foot. We look to pressure and pick the ball when we can. This must be taught at your scout team training session.
  - What is his strength in the air?
  - How is the quality of his first touch?
  - Assess his foot speed without the ball.
  - Is he strong in the air?
  - What defender looks to start the attack and which defenders step forward into the attack?
  - Who tracks well and who does not?

In regard to assessing **midfielders** I look for touch and speed on the ball, quickness away from the ball, vision, and level of fitness.

Questions To Be Answered:
- Which midfielders get forward quickly and who are the first to retreat defensively?
- You must decide which midfielders can maintain possession under pressure and which ones lose possession in this situation.
- When a midfielder receives quick and steady pressure does he turn and play the ball back to his defenders?
- Find the midfielders who can wall pass themselves through and get numbers forward and the midfielders who will use a penetration pass to split your defense.
- Which midfielders make penetrating or overlapping runs?
- Once again, who tracks well and who does not?

Strikers, front runners, or wingers used in any combination are addressed in the following manner.

Questions To Be Answered:
- Again, assess foot speed off the ball and level of fitness.
- How is their first touch?
- Which ones possess the ability to beat defenders 1 v 1 and 1 v 2?
- Which front runner can serve crosses?
- Who can get on the tail end of a cross?
- Who is dangerous in the box; on the flanks?
- Are their movements and dribbling moves predictable?
- Can they play with their back to the goal?
- Are they predominately one footed? (Remember Pelé used one foot most of the time. His 'weak foot' caused considerable damage to his opponents as well.)
- What types of runs does each make?
- Who can possess the ball long enough so they can get numbers forward into the attack?
- Which attacker will track a defender stepping forward?

It is at this point that you should begin to look at match-ups. These are first impressions and should be reviewed after the match. Who matches well with the weak link defender? Who defends their best striker, etc?

As a substitute enters the match write down the number of the player entering for the number exiting (#2 for #10). This helps with your organization so you do not miss a mark. Many times match-ups change when substitutes enter the field.

THE ATTACK-TACTICS, THUMB INDEX, • A, AT - Pages 21-22.

(The Attack has five separate thumb indexes to increase the speed and efficiency in collecting information.) During the course of the match you are scouting you must answer two critical tactical questions: First, where does the point of attack originate? The answer to this is aided by a team's style of play. I also add one style I have observed as I watch American soccer. I call it Direct Forward Without Intent. Too many American teams bang the ball forward and then try to gain possession in the attacking third. Begin to diagram successful attacks mounted by your opponents using the Key To Diagrams on page 20. Also, pay attention to where their attack stalls and why. The second question, who initiates (starts) the attack: this is usually the playmaker. Figure out where he gets the ball from and who is giving it to him. If you close his source quickly in a match he will become very ineffective. Look for any adjustments made by the opposing staff to compensate for this. If you can apply pressure to the playmaker and force the ball backwards you have changed the origin of the point of the attack. When you accomplish this you begin to dominate possession.

THE ATTACK • CORNER KICKS, THUMB INDEX • AC - Page 23.

(Use the Key To Diagrams on page 20)

A high percentage of goals are scored worldwide from corner kicks and free kicks. There are many teams who cannot mount a successful attack but are efficient in these facets of the game. It is important to identify each player and his exact positioning on the field using uniform numbers for both corners and free kicks.

Questions To Be Answered:
- Does the same server take the corners from both sides?
- Does he use the same foot from both sides?
- When you mark the flight of the ball is it an inswinger or outswinger? Where does it land?
- Is the ball driven or floated into the box?
- Are short corners taken?
- Is it played near post, far post, or to the penalty spot?
- Is the ball played near and flicked to the far post?
- Chart the runs of all attackers. Are some runs dummy runs? Mark the starting and ending position of each run. Are players positioned on the top of the box for loose balls?
- Do any defenders move forward for corners? Who is left to defend? Can you counter quickly?
- Do they place anyone on the goalkeeper? Does the goalkeeper get a clear path to the ball?

THE ATTACK • FREE KICKS, THUMB INDEX • AF - Page 24.
(Use the Key To Diagrams on page 20)

Once again, mark the exact positioning of players over the ball and around the penalty area.

Questions To Be Answered:
- At what distance do their free kicks pose a threat of scoring?
- Do they take quick free kicks in the middle third of the field? If they do - how do they get their numbers forward? (Example - down the flanks)

When free kicks are taken near or in the box:

- How many players are over the ball?
- Which foot does each player shoot with? Inside or outside of foot?
- Are there dummy runs over the ball?
- Is the ball ever passed to someone making a run over the ball?
- What combinations do they perform over the ball?
- What type of combination play is used with players away from the ball? (Example - walling a player to finish)
- Are they quick and organized when taking free kicks?
- When a shot is taken is it bent over the wall or driven?
- What was the location the shooter was aiming for?
- Do they float balls in? If so, who was at the tail end of the service?
- What position on the field do they float balls into the box and from what position do they shoot?
- Do they take advantage of quick sets if the opposing team is slow to defend?
- Which attackers off the ball work hard in the box for any rebounds?
- On indirect free kicks pressure should always be applied to the shooter. Figure out the best approach for this.

THE ATTACK - THROW-INS, GOAL KICKS, KICKOFFS, THUMB INDEX • AT - Page 25.
(Use the Key To Diagrams on page 20)

THROW-INS. Our major concern is throw-ins in the attacking third.

Questions To Be Answered:
- Are there players in an offside position?

- Do players make runs to an offside position to receive the ball?
- Do players check to or away from the thrower? Are they creating space for themselves or teammates?
- What is the distance the ball can be thrown?
- Is the field size comparable to the field you will be playing on?
- Do they set-up as if it were a corner kick (set play) for long throws into the box?
- Do they flick the ball to the far post?

GOAL KICKS. Our major concern is their predictability on goal kicks.
Questions To Be Answered:
- Do they stand to receive all goal kicks?
- Do they move to create space for themselves or teammates?
- Do they flood an area with players to gain possession?
- Do they flick the ball forward to a target?
- Do they play any short goal kicks?
- What is the distance of the long goal kicks? Are they played to a predictable spot?

KICKOFFS. Our major concern is either their predictability or set plays from a kickoff.

Questions To Be Answered:
- Does your opponent kickoff in the same sequence each time?
  (Example - backpass to center midfield) If so, how can you defend it and regain possession?
- How do they build from the kickoff? Many times style of play dictates this.
- Are their set plays in a predictable sequence?

- Are they composed after scoring a goal or are they vulnerable because of a lack of composure? Too much excitement can work in a negative way for a team.

THE ATTACK - SCORING OPPORTU-NITIES, THUMB INDEX • SO - Page 26. In this section of the guide you want to chart the precise movements that led to a scoring opportunity or goal. (Use the Key To Diagrams on page 20)

Questions To Be Answered:
- Where did the goal scoring opportunity originate from and with whom?
- How many times did the same opportunity occur?
- Is the manner in which it develops predictable? How can you shut down this opportunity?
- What type of service or combination led to the opportunity?
- What type of runs led to the opportunity?
- What part of the body (foot, head) did the shot come from?
  What corner was the shooter aiming for?

PENALTY KICKS - SHOOTER AND KEEPER, THUMB INDEX • PK - Page 27 (Use the Key provided on the Penalty Kick page 27)

If you are lucky you may see a penalty kick. Many games are won and lost on a single penalty kick. Also, advancement in a tournament is many times determined by penalty kick shootouts.

The chart and key describe the method of recording the penalty shot. Many penalty kick shooters are predictable as to what foot, what part of the foot, and what side and corner they will shoot to.

The Goalkeeper Defending PK Chart has simple fill-in and yes/no answers.

Questions To Be Answered:
- What was the score of the game at the time the PK was taken? If the game was in hand many times a coach will not give away any secrets and a secondary shooter may be implemented.
- Do the score and the amount of time remaining in the game appear to add pressure to the primary shooter or is he poised?
- If it is the primary shooter, does everything about the penalty kick seem automatic?

PENALTY KICKS FOR ADVANCEMENT IN TOURNAMENT PLAY.

Most coaches have a definite order for their shooters. Fortune is on your side if you are able to see a penalty kick shootout. Always review the information gained with your goalkeeper but do not require him to memorize the information. You will have the scouting guide on your bench during the match. During the prep time before and between each shot give your goalkeeper hand signals. Read the information in the guide, touch the leg the shooter uses, and point to the corner he prefers. Remember, your side is the opposite of the goalkeeper because he is facing you. Also, emulate this scenario in a training session.

THE DEFENSE - TACTICS, THUMB INDEX • D, DT - Pages 28-29
(Use the Key To Diagrams on page 20)

You must look at the defense as a whole unit and as pieces of a puzzle. First, how do they collectively defend? And, as discussed before, where are the weak links you can exploit. On the full field diagram illustrate how they defend within whatever system of play they use.

Questions To Be Answered:
- Defensively, are they organized? Disciplined?
- Are they composed under pressure? Are they composed after a goal is scored against them?
- Is there leadership and direction? Who does this come from?
- Do they get numbers in behind the ball?
- Do they defend with eleven (11) players?
- Where is their line of defense drawn? Are there efforts to funnel the ball into a weak link player? Do they try to funnel the ball away from the playmaker?
- Do they defend - Goal side/Ball side?
- Do they track well?

Sweeper/Stopper System
- How well does the sweeper read the game? Does he have the vision to see midfielders pushing into the attack? Does he demand that these runs are tracked and marked goal side?
- Does the sweeper become compact and flat? If so, when?
- Does the sweeper get sucked to the outside?
- What is the cushion of space between the sweeper and stopper (How much depth does he provide?) Can you exploit that space with diagonal runs?
- Is there space behind the flank defenders to penetrate into?

Does he demand that these runs are tracked and marked goal side?

- Does the sweeper become compact and flat? If so, when?
- Does the sweeper get sucked to the outside?
- What is the cushion of space between the sweeper and stopper (How much depth does he provide?) Can you exploit that space with diagonal runs?
- Is there space behind the flank defenders to penetrate into?

Flat Back System

- Does each player know his function within the system? Are they organized?
- Do they stay compact? Too compact?
- Can you split them with penetration passes? Can you spread them with runs on the flanks?
- Do they provide pressure and cover on the ball?
- Does the goalkeeper cover the space behind the defenders well? Can the goalkeeper use his feet well? Which is his dominant foot?
- Do the central defenders and defensive central midfielders force the ball to the flanks?
- Which midfielders provide support to the backs?
- When they regain possession does the defense open up quickly?

Man to Man Marking System

- How tight is their marking? In America many times man to man marking is taken literally. Players follow players everywhere and are "stuck" to them. If this is so, can you exploit this? Can you take defenders away and create space for runs into this space?

- Do the weak side defenders provide balance? If not, can you penetrate into this space?

Zonal Defense

- How are they organized within zones?
- Do they communicate well enough to pass players on?
- Do they track diagonal runs through zones?
- How do they defend when the attacking team gets numbers up in a zone?
- Can the zones be spread and can you find seams between the zones?

High and Low Pressure

- Too many American teams try to play high pressure all match. If your opponent does, two key elements must be evaluated. What is their level of fitness and what will the temperature be at game time when you play them?
- For either type of pressure you must answer: when do they switch, where do they switch, and for how long a duration do they maintain a specific pressure?
  (Example - Do they high pressure right after they have scored a goal?)

Offsides Trap

- First identify if they use this tactic. If they do, answer where and when do they use it?
- Is the trap done efficiently and with direction?
- You must decide where and how to beat the trap.

THE DEFENSE - CORNER KICKS, FREE KICKS, PENALTY KICKS, KICK-OFFS, THUMB INDEX • DC - page 30.

Defending Corner Kicks. Please take note that many times a team that plays man to man during the match may play zonal defense on corners and visa versa. Some teams will play a combination of zone and man to man. Write down uniform numbers of players in their respective positions prior to the corner. You may find strikers who are strong in the air coming back to defend.

Questions To Be Answered:
- How organized is their team?
- How many players do they defend the corner with?
- Do they defend a short corner?
- Are the players on the posts doing an efficient job?
  Many coaches put players on the posts but never teach them the function of that task.
- Is this a team who battles in the box?
- Do they let the ball bounce in the box? The team that lets the ball bounce in either box usually cannot defend well in the air and cannot score goals from the air.
- Does the goalkeeper take control of the box?
- Upon the goalkeeper regaining possession how quickly do they counter? From this information you must refine or develop set plays from which you can score.

Defending Free Kicks. Again, observe how they mark during set pieces from different distances from goal. You want to evaluate the information gained and exploit their weakness for an opportunity that will result in a goal.

Questions To Be Answered:
- Are they organized?
- Who sets the wall - goalkeeper or field player?
- Is it set accurately and with speed? Is it constructed well?
- Is the proper number of players placed in the wall for all situations?
- How do they defend players not over the ball?
- Do they put immediate pressure on the shooter?
- Does the goalkeeper control the box?
- How quickly do they counter after regaining possession?

Defending Penalty Kicks. Defending a PK requires a definite strategy. Teams that do not defend well may have a keeper make a great save, give up a rebound, only to have it knocked home.

Questions To Be Answered:
- Do they place a player on each corner of the "D"?
- Are players assigned to cover the sides of the penalty area? Many saves are pushed in this direction.
- Do they mark each attacking player man to man?

Defending Kick-Offs. Regaining possession from a kickoff is a team effort and must be well executed.

Questions To Be Answered:
- How do they pressure the ball?
- Where do they pressure the ball?
- Are they forcing the ball in a specific direction for a definite reason?

PREPARING FOR A TEAM MEETING
AND A SCOUT TEAM TRAINING SESSION

Now begins the time in which you must incorporate all of the **Questions To Be Answered** into one complete synopsis. Simply said, find the answers to the questions and you will Find A Way To Win! At this juncture pages 15, 16, 21, and 28 should be completed. During this period continuously look for the weaknesses of your opponent. Circle these areas. Contemplate how to attack every technical or tactical breakdown. For each deficiency write within the circle how you want your team to take advantage of the situation. Next, go back through the guide and draw a rectangle around the major strengths of your opponent. This time you must prepare your team to neutralize either a specific player(s) or some component of their team tactics. Again, inside each retangular write down how you want your team to accomplish this.

It is time to review their individual player personnel. Remember, early in the text you were asked to think of ideal match-ups on a player for player basis. Review these match-ups and make the necessary changes now that you have seen the entire picture. Be prepared to make changes at game time in the event that at kickoff one of your players or theirs is injured. A back-up match-up plan is important. During preseason and inseason training sessions you should experiment with players in different roles. The complexion in a team changes drastically when a major change is made. You do not want your team's mental attitude to be one of fear because you have not prepared them for possible role changes. Your job is to guide your team to composure. Also, as the match begins take a serious look as to how these match-ups are progressing. How quickly we monitor and adjust can be the difference in the game.

You now have prepared a technical and tactical game plan for your team. Your preparation of the Team Meeting Prep Sheet (page 31) is the next step. Write in the necessary information in a simplistic manner that will guide your team through the meeting. Do not overburden your team with complex terminology. Photocopy the completed Prep Sheet and distribute to your team upon assemblance of your meeting. This is why I discussed earlier that it would be beneficial to both you and your team to scout a preseason match and go through this entire process. Understanding what is expected and keeping a uniform approach to each match is what premier athletes should be accustomed to.

The blackboard is an integral part of the team meeting. Prior to your players' arrival write on the board the uniform numbers of the opposition's starters in their respective positions. This gives your team an instant familiarity with the players and how they are placed into a system. Also, discuss the roles of any substitutes. This helps because many times match-ups change when a substitute enters the field. Use the blackboard as a visual and show various components, such as how they attack, the various runs, etc…

Encourage your players to ask questions at any time during the meeting. They are, after all, the solution. This allows them to become in tune with the final preparation. From the team meeting your team should be adjourning to the field to continue preparation with the scout team.

Developing Your Scout Team For a Training Session

Prior to the team meeting you should select which one of your substitutes or 'B' Team players will fill the roles of your opponents. As the session unfolds use your substitutes with the 'A' Team so they will understand what is expected of them and so they know they are also part of the solution. Identify which of your 'B' team players is taking the role of a specific opponent. Pinnies with uniform numbers pressed on alleviates this problem. Discuss with individual 'B' team players how to mimic precisely the movements of players on the opposing team. For example, if a flank midfielder makes a certain run have the 'B' team player do this run in the training game. Walk your team through where they will see technical and tactical breakdowns. Show them how to attack these situations. Also, go through all of your opponent's dead ball situations with the scout team movements identical to your opponents. Equally important, discuss your opponents strengths and walk your team through how to counter them. The final product in your training session should be an 11 v 11 game at match pace under these simulated circumstances. A comment about field size - set up the length and width of the field so it will be similar to the field you are playing your opponent on. You can do this with small cones. This will definitely help your team learn how to either close down space or play on a large field. The game and all practices should end, as always, on a positive note. At the end of the training session your team should leave the field with a confident understanding of what is expected of them and **How To Win!**

Game Day - Pregame - Locker Room

You have already discussed in length how to attack and defend your opponent. During your pregame discussion you should devote part of the time to reviewing the major objectives of your game plan. Do not begin to re-dissect your opponent. This was the focus of the team meeting. The pregame comments you make should be to re-focus the team to the game plan.

Game Day - Field - Warm-up

Select this time as each player is warming up either individually or with a partner to walk around the field. Give brief comments to each player. An example would be, 'Alan, make sure you force #3 to load the ball on his left foot.' This helps to reinforce many of the individual tasks required to glue together the pieces of the puzzle. Also, study your opponent's warm-up. You may observe their back-up keeper as the starter. Why he is playing is not the issue. You must quickly evaluate his technical ability. Look for any detail (example, a key player in street clothes) that would better prepare you for kickoff.

The Match

As soon as the match begins you must quickly assess your opponent. Are they adhering to the game plan you previously watched and evaluated? Are the match-ups you developed working? Minor adjustments must be made without haste. Many times giving direction to a team leader on the field is the fix. If an early substitution is required prep him briefly before he enters the field with the necessary adjustment and how you would like it to be accomplished. Any team adjustment should be made at halftime.

Teams that do not scout usually are forced to make major adjustments during the course of the first half and then a few more at halftime. Because you spent the time scouting and doing your homework you have prepared your team well and you have given them the knowledge, preparation, and confidence which will allow them to **Find A Way To Win**!

Good Luck, Be Dedicated, and Win!

PART 2

Joe Bertuzzi's
Soccer Scouting Guide

There are four (4) blank scouting guides
included. You will now be better
prepared to **WIN!**

Joe Bertuzzi's
Soccer Scounting Guide

_____Scout Guide

TEAM NAME

For The Season of 20____

vs

_____   _____

Away Opponent   **Home Opponent**

_____   _____

Field Size   **Condition of the Field**

_____   _____

Kickoff Time   **Weather Conditions**

_____   _____

Halftime Score   **Final Score**

_____   _____

Date: **Prepared By:**

Goalkeeper PreGame Assessment

_____GK is/is not in set position prior to shot

———GK does/does not take attacking step

———GK does/does not properly cut down angle

Collapse Dive Technique
_____
_____

Extension Dive Technique
_____
_____

Handling of Crosses
_____
_____

Parrying Balls
_____
_____

Boxing Balls
_____
_____

Tipping Balls
_____
_____

Breakaway Saves
_____
_____

Distribution
_____
_____

GK Strengths
_____
_____

GK Weaknesses
_____
_____

Team System of Play

System of Play

Key Players within the System

Weak Links within the System

System of Play - Players within the System

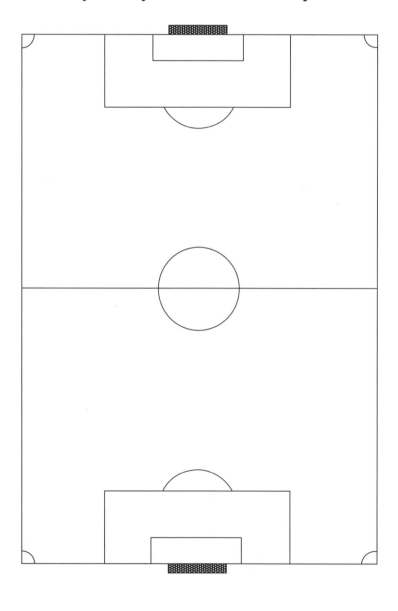

Individual Player Assessments

Players Who Need Special Attention

_____

Weak Link Players

_____

Coaches Notes:

_____

_____

_____

_____

_____

_____

_____

_____

_____

_____

Individual Player Assessments

Goalkeeper	#	Jersey Color	Name

Technical/Tactical Observations:

Strengths:

Weaknesses:

Position	#	Name	Left/Right Foot

Technical/Tactical Observations:

Strengths:

Weaknesses:

Position	#	Name	Left/Right Foot

Technical/Tactical Observations:

Strengths:

Weaknesses:

Position	#	Name	Left/Right Foot

Technical/Tactical Observations:

Strengths:

Weaknesses:

Position	#	Name	Left/Right Foot

Technical/Tactical Observations:

Strengths:

Weaknesses:

Individual Player Assessments

Position   #   Name   Left/Right Foot
Technical/Tactical Observations:

Strengths:
Weaknesses:

Position   #   Name   Left/Right Foot
Technical/Tactical Observations:

Strengths:
Weaknesses:

Position   #   Name   Left/Right Foot
Technical/Tactical Observations:

Strengths:
Weaknesses:

Position   #   Name   Left/Right Foot
Technical/Tactical Observations:

Strengths:
Weaknesses:

Position   #   Name   Left/Right Foot
Technical/Tactical Observations:

Strengths:
Weaknesses:

Position   #   Name   Left/Right Foot
Technical/Tactical Observations:

Strengths:
Weaknesses:

Individual Player Assessments Substitutes

Position   #   Name   Left/Right Foot
Technical/Tactical Observations:

Strengths:
Weaknesses:

Position   #   Name   Left/Right Foot
Technical/Tactical Observations:

Strengths:
Weaknesses:

Position   #   Name   Left/Right Foot
Technical/Tactical Observations:

Strengths:
Weaknesses:

Position   #   Name   Left/Right Foot
Technical/Tactical Observations:

Strengths:
Weaknesses:

Position   #   Name   Left/Right Foot
Technical/Tactical Observations:

Strengths:
Weaknesses:

Position   #   Name   Left/Right Foot
Technical/Tactical Observations:

Strengths:
Weaknesses:

Key to Diagrams

X = Attacker

O = Defender

- - - - - - - - -▶   = Movement of Ball

───────────▶   = Movement of Player

∿∿∿∿➘   = Movement of Player Dribbling the Ball

⌒➘   = Curved Shot or Service

   = Circled number is the location a player has scored from

10.   = A dot next to a number is where the ball is located prior to a set piece

The Attack

_____ Direct Style of Play

_____ Indirect Style of Play

_____Direct Forward Without Intent

Key Players to Mark on Corners

_____

Key Players to Mark on Free Kicks

_____

Key Players Over the Ball on Free Kicks

_____

Players(s) with a Long Throw-in_____

Coaches Notes:

_____

_____

_____

_____

_____

_____

_____

_____

_____

_____

The Attack - Tactics

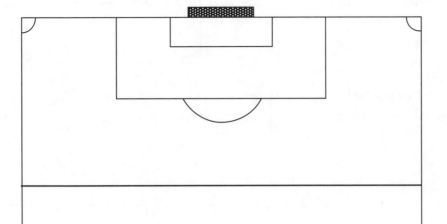

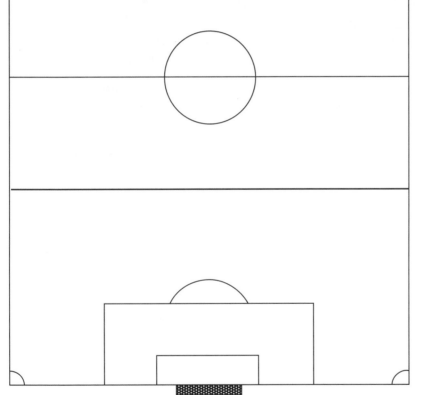

Attacking Third

Middle Third

Defensive Third

1) Where does the point of attack originate?

_____

2) Who initiates (starts) the attack?

_____

3) Who does the playmaker primarily get the ball from?

_____

The Attack - Corner Kicks

Coaches Notes:

_____

_____

_____

_____

_____

_____

_____

_____

_____

The Attack - Free Kicks

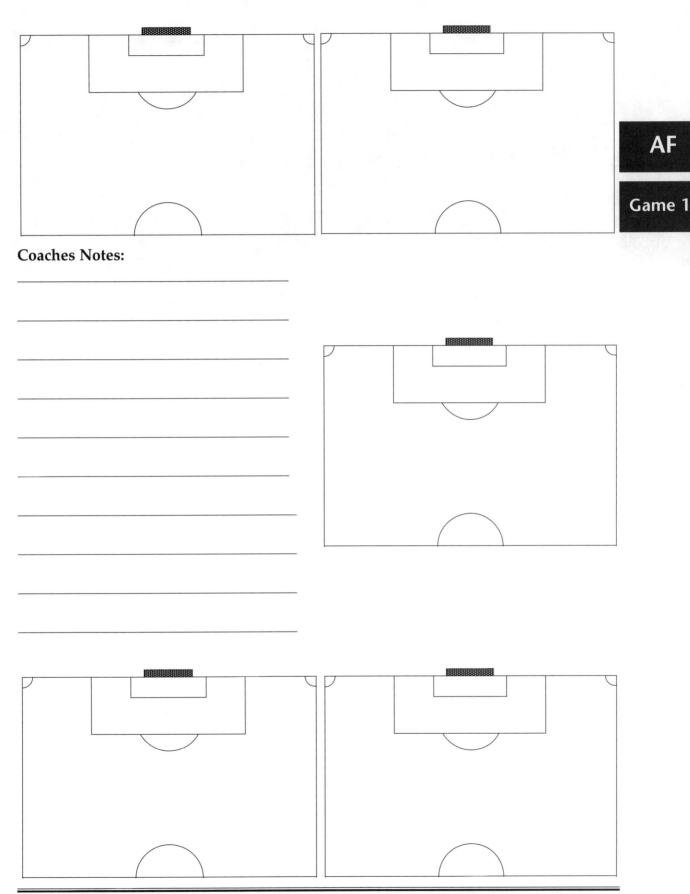

Coaches Notes:

_____

_____

_____

_____

_____

_____

_____

_____

_____

_____

The Attack - Throw-ins

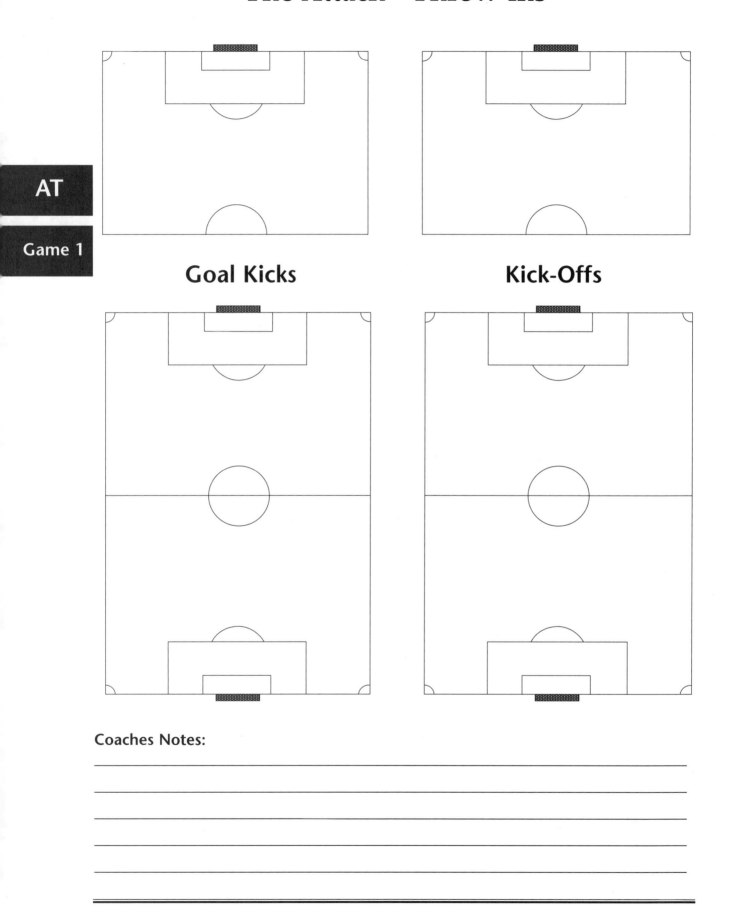

Goal Kicks

Kick-Offs

Coaches Notes:

_____

_____

_____

_____

_____

The Attack - Scoring Opportunities

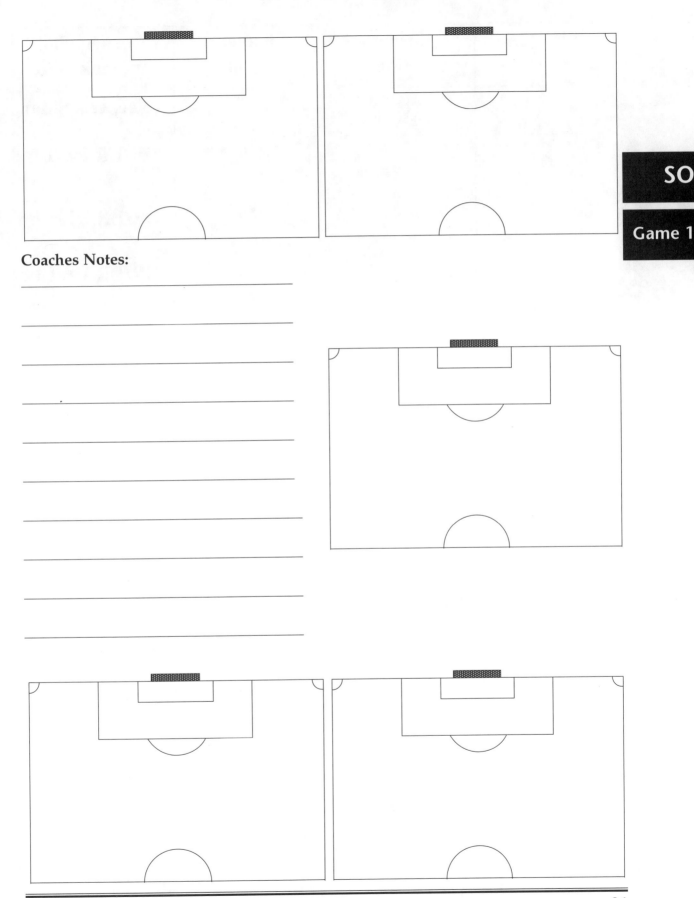

Coaches Notes:

_____

_____

_____

_____

_____

_____

_____

_____

_____

Penalty Kicks

Shooter	Keeper's Side	Shooter's Foot	Corner Shot was taken to
	Shot Was Taken To		(Keeper's Side)
#	R/L	R/L	UR/LR UL/LL
#	R/L	R/L	UR/LR UL/LL
#	R/L	R/L	UR/LR UL/LL
#	R/L	R/L	UR/LR UL/LL
#	R/L	R/L	UR/LR UL/LL

Key To Penalty Kicks
R = Right
L = Left
UR = Upper Right
LR = Lower Right
UL = Upper Left
LL = Lower Left

Coaches Notes:_____
_____
_____
_____
_____
_____
_____
_____

Goalkeeper Defending PK:

Range to Post_____

Better Diving Side_____

Does he Read the Shooter or Pick A Side_____

Is he Poised Prior to the Shot_____

The Defense

_____Sweeper Stopper System

_____Flat Back System (3 Defenders/4 Defenders)

_____Man to Man Marking System

_____Zonal Defense Marking System

_____Side Team Funnels To_____

_____High Pressure - What Times During Match

        _____
        _____
        _____

_____Low Pressure - What Times During Match

        _____
        _____
        _____

_____Offsides Trap - Where and When

        _____
        _____
        _____

The Defense - Tactics

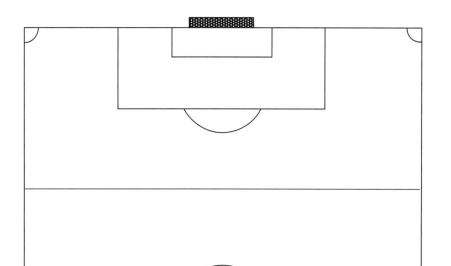

Attacking Third

Middle Third

Defensive Third

1) Where do they draw their line of defense?

_____

2) Regardless of the system of play, do they track well?

_____

3) How well do they pressure the ball and how many numbers do they get in behind the ball?_____

The Defense - Corner Kicks

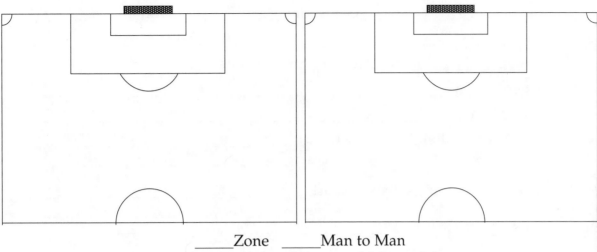

_____Zone   _____Man to Man
_____Combination of Zone and Man to Man

Free Kicks

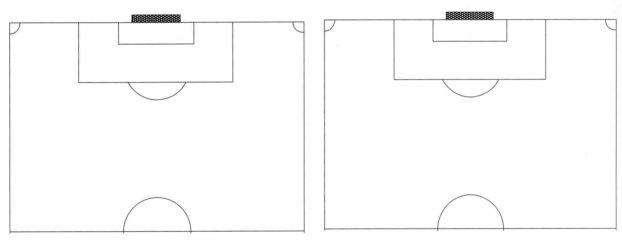

1. #_____Sets the Wall   2. Organized/Not Organized in Setting Wall
3. Fast/Slow in Setting Wall   4. Pressured/No Pressure on Ball

Penalty Kicks   # Kick Offs

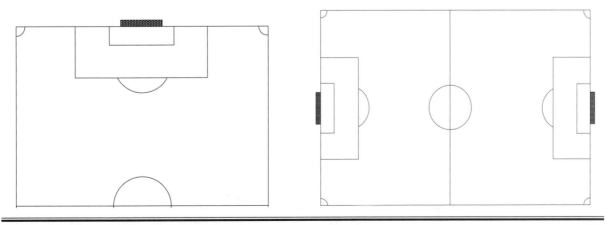

Team Meeting Prep Sheet

Date of Game_____Game Time_____Location _____

Opponent_____Size of Field _____

Summary of Opponents Strengths and Weaknesses

System of Play_____

Style of Play_____

Key Players within System   Attack:_____

                                    Defense:_____

Weak Links within System   Attack:_____

                                    Defense:_____

Goalkeeping _____

Key Players to Mark on Corners _____

Key Players to Mark on Free Kicks _____

Player(s) with a Long Throw-in _____

Penalty Kick Shooter _____

Defending   1. Sweeper Stopper or Flat Back System 3/4

             _____

             2. Man to Man Marking or Zonal System

             _____

             Side Team Funnels to_____

             Types of Pressure and When They Are Used _____

             _____

             Offsides Trap_____

How Team Defends: Corners _____

                    Free Kicks _____

                    Penalty Kicks _____

                    Kick-Offs _____

Overall Team Strengths _____

Overall Team Weaknesses _____

Keys to Victory   1. _____

                2. _____

                3. _____

Player Comments_____

_____

TM

Game 1

Joe Bertuzzi's
Soccer Scounting Guide

_____Scout Guide

TEAM NAME

For The Season of 20____

vs

_____   _____

Away Opponent   **Home Opponent**

_____

Field Size   **Conditions of the Field**

_____

Kickoff Time   **Weather Conditions**

_____

Halftime Score   **Final Score**

_____

Date: **Prepared By:**

Goalkeeper Pregame Assessment

_____GK is/is not in set position prior to shot

——GK does/does not take attacking step

——GK does/does not properly cut down angle

Collapse Dive Technique

_____

_____

Extension Dive Technique

_____

_____

Handling of Crosses

_____

_____

Parrying Balls

_____

_____

Boxing Balls

_____

_____

Tipping Balls

_____

_____

Breakaway Saves

_____

_____

Distribution

_____

_____

GK Strengths

_____

_____

GK Weaknesses

_____

_____

Team System of Play

System of Play

Key Players within the System

Weak Links within the System .

System of Play - Players within the System

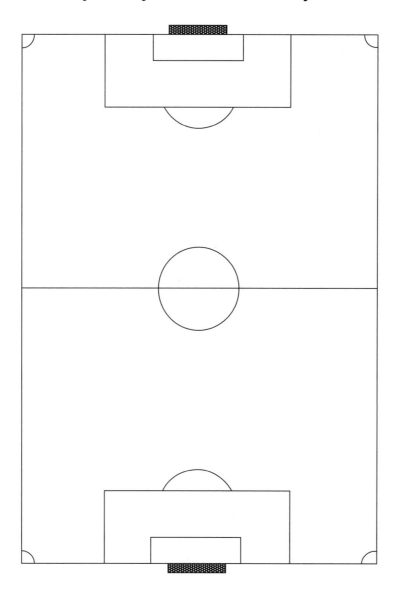

Individual Player Assessments

Players who need Special Attention

_____

Weak Link Players

_____

Coaches Notes:

_____

_____

_____

_____

_____

_____

_____

_____

_____

PA

Game 2

Goalkeeper   #   Jersey Color   Name

Technical/Tactical Observations:

Strengths:

Weaknesses:

Position   #   Name   Left/Right Foot

Technical/Tactical Observations:

Strengths:

Weaknesses:

Position   #   Name   Left/Right Foot

Technical/Tactical Observations:

Strengths:

Weaknesses:

Position   #   Name   Left/Right Foot

Technical/Tactical Observations:

Strengths:

Weaknesses:

Position   #   Name   Left/Right Foot

Technical/Tactical Observations:

Strengths:

Weaknesses:

Individual Player Assessments

Starting Team

Position   #   Name   Left/Right Foot

Technical/Tactical Observations:

Strengths:

Weaknesses:

Position   #   Name   Left/Right Foot

Technical/Tactical Observations:

Strengths:

Weaknesses:

Position   #   Name   Left/Right Foot

Technical/Tactical Observations:

Strengths:

Weaknesses:

Position   #   Name   Left/Right Foot

Technical/Tactical Observations:

Strengths:

Weaknesses:

Position   #   Name   Left/Right Foot

Technical/Tactical Observations:

Strengths:

Weaknesses:

Position   #   Name   Left/Right Foot

Technical/Tactical Observations:

Strengths:

Weaknesses:

PA

Game 2

Position	#	Name	Left/Right Foot

Technical/Tactical Observations:

Strengths:

Weaknesses:

Position	#	Name	Left/Right Foot

Technical/Tactical Observations:

Strengths:

Weaknesses:

Position	#	Name	Left/Right Foot

Technical/Tactical Observations:

Strengths:

Weaknesses:

Position	#	Name	Left/Right Foot

Technical/Tactical Observations:

Strengths:

Weaknesses:

Position	#	Name	Left/Right Foot

Technical/Tactical Observations:

Strengths:

Weaknesses:

Position	#	Name	Left/Right Foot

Technical/Tactical Observations:

Strengths:

Weaknesses:

Key to Diagrams

X = Attacker

O = Defender

- - - - - - - → = Movement of Ball

———————→ = Movement of Player

∿∿∿∿→ = Movement of Player Dribbling the Ball

⌒ = Curved Shot or Service

 = Circled number is the location a player has scored from

10. = A dot next to a number is where the ball is located prior to a set piece

The Attack

_____Direct Style of Play

_____Indirect Style of Play

_____Direct Forward Without Intent

Key Players to Mark on Corners

_____

Key Players to Mark on Free Kicks

_____

Key Players Over the Ball on Free Kicks

_____

Players(s) with a Long Throw-in_____

Coaches Notes:

_____

_____

_____

_____

_____

_____

_____

_____

The Attack - Tactics

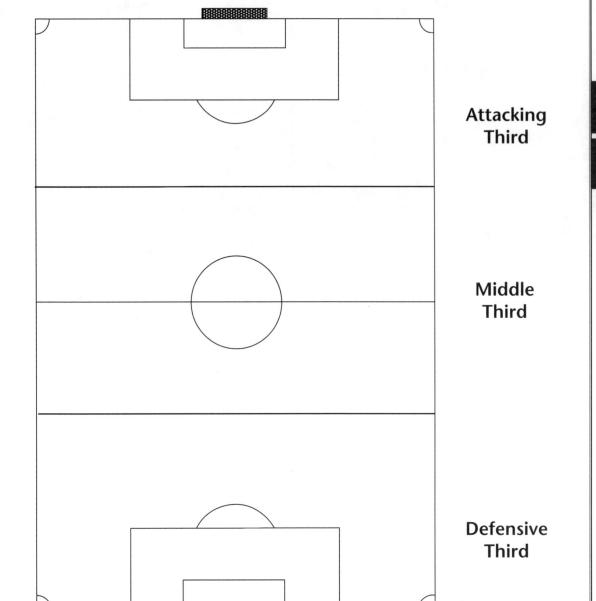

Attacking
Third

Middle
Third

Defensive
Third

1) Where does the point of attack originate?

_____

2) Who initiates (starts) the attack?

_____

3) Who does the playmaker primarily get the ball from?

_____

The Attack - Corner Kicks

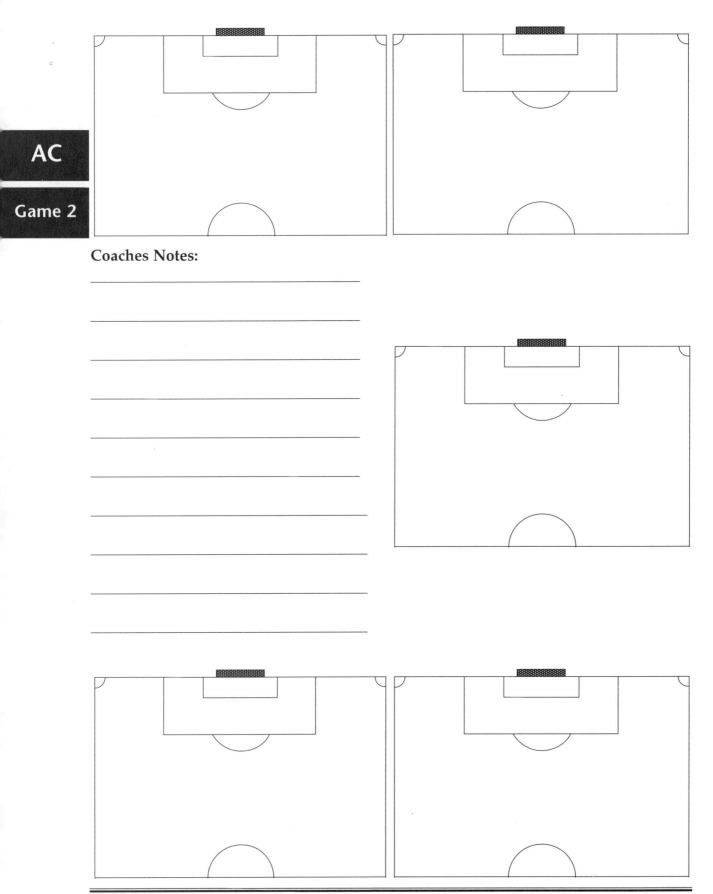

Coaches Notes:

_____

_____

_____

_____

_____

_____

_____

_____

_____

_____

The Attack - Free Kicks

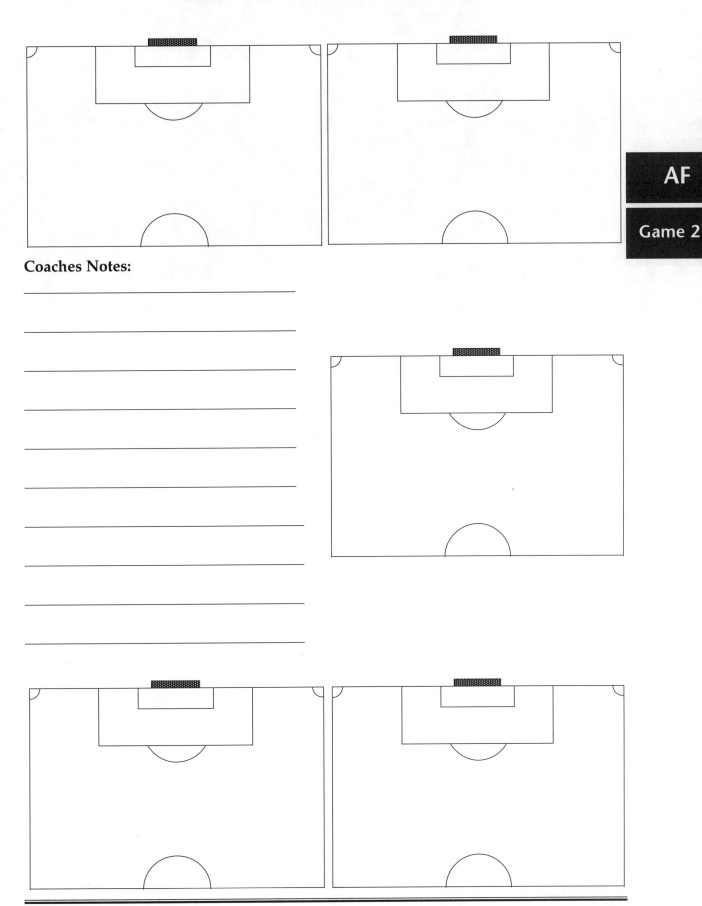

Coaches Notes:

_____

_____

_____

_____

_____

_____

_____

_____

_____

_____

AF

Game 2

The Attack - Throw-ins

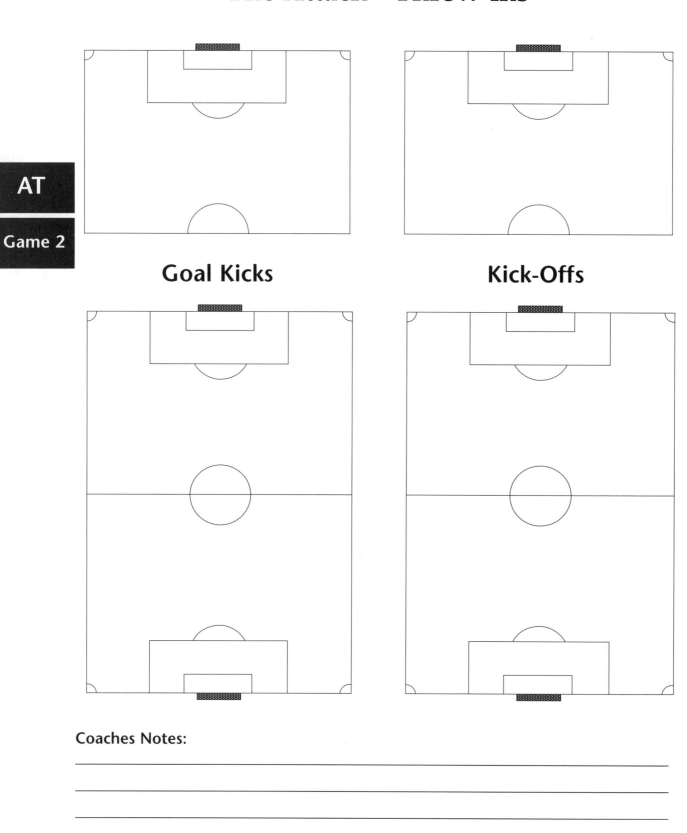

Goal Kicks

Kick-Offs

Coaches Notes:

_____

_____

_____

_____

_____

The Attack - Scoring Opportunities

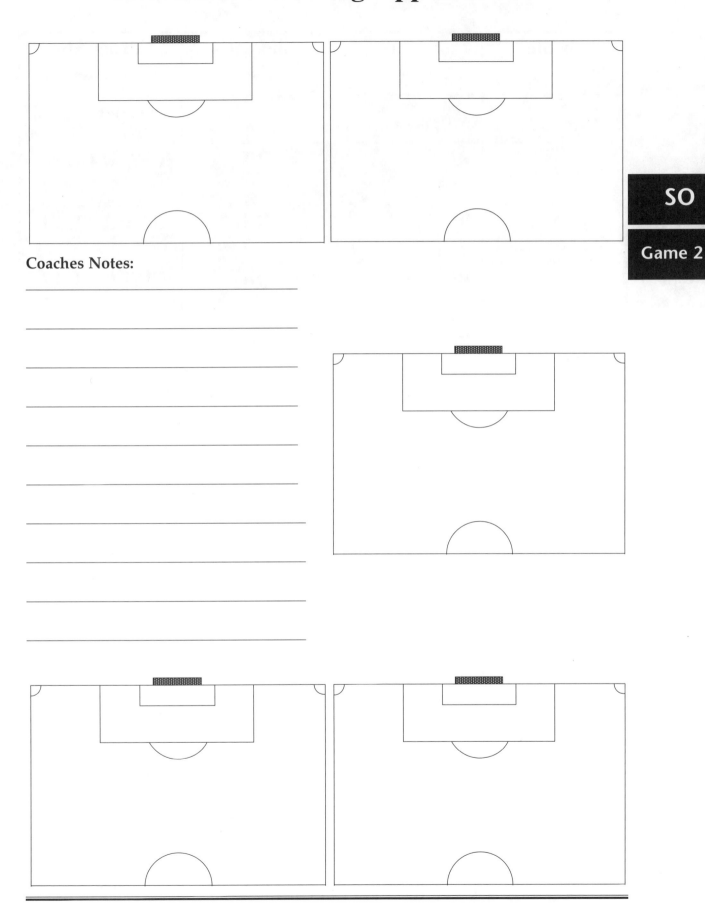

Coaches Notes:

_____

_____

_____

_____

_____

_____

_____

_____

Penalty Kicks

Shooter	Keeper's Side	Shooter's Foot	Corner Shot was taken to
	Shot Was Taken To		(Keeper's Side)
#	R/L	R/L	UR/LR UL/LL
#	R/L	R/L	UR/LR UL/LL
#	R/L	R/L	UR/LR UL/LL
#	R/L	R/L	UR/LR UL/LL
#	R/L	R/L	UR/LR UL/LL

Key To Penalty Kicks
R = Right
L = Left
UR = Upper Right
LR = Lower Right
UL = Upper Left
LL = Lower Left

Coaches Notes:_____
_____
_____
_____
_____
_____
_____
_____

Goalkeeper Defending PK:

Range to Post_____

Better Diving Side_____

Does he Read the Shooter or Pick A Side_____

Is he Poised Prior to the Shot_____

The Defense

_____Sweeper Stopper System

_____Flat Back System (3 Defenders/4 Defenders)

_____Man to Man Marking System

_____Zonal Defense Marking System

_____Side Team Funnels To_____

_____High Pressure - What Times During Match

           _____

           _____

           _____

_____Low Pressure - What Times During Match

           _____

           _____

           _____

_____Offsides Trap - Where and When

           _____

           _____

           _____

D

Game 2

The Defense - Tactics

Attacking Third

Middle Third

Defensive Third

1) Where do they draw their line of defense?
_____

2) Regardless of the system of play, do they track well?
_____

3) How well do they pressure the ball and how many numbers do they get in behind the ball?_____

The Defense - Corner Kicks

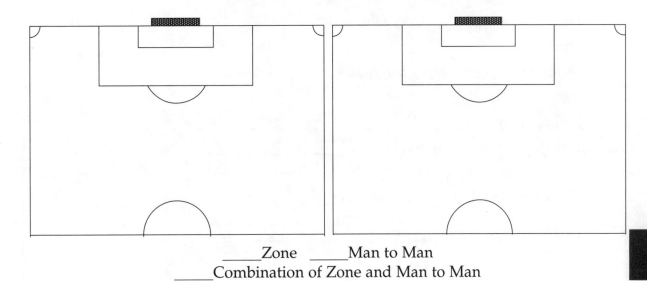

_____Zone _____Man to Man
_____Combination of Zone and Man to Man

Free Kicks

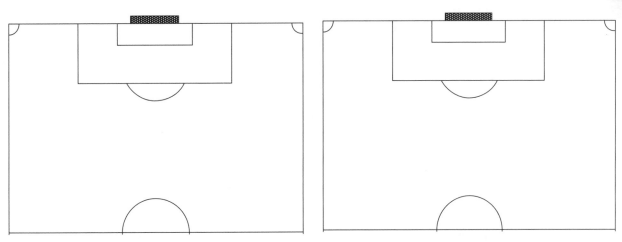

1. #_____Sets the Wall   2. Organized/Not Organized in Setting Wall
3. Fast/Slow in Setting Wall   4. Pressured/No Pressure on Ball

Penalty Kicks   # Kick Offs

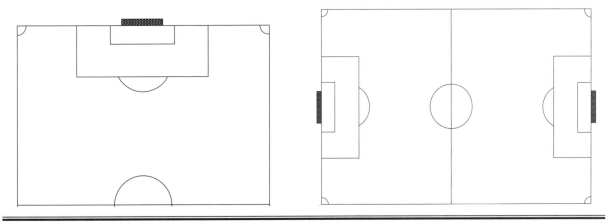

Team Meeting Prep Sheet

Date of Game_____Game Time_____Location _____

Opponent_____Size of Field _____

Summary of Opponents Strengths and Weaknesses

System of Play_____

Style of Play_____

Key Players within System   Attack:_____

                                 Defense:_____

Weak Links within System   Attack:_____

                                 Defense:_____

Goalkeeping _____

Key Players to Mark on Corners _____

Key Players to Mark on Free Kicks _____

Player(s) with a Long Throw-in _____

Penalty Kick Shooter _____

Defending   1. Sweeper Stopper or Flat Back System 3/4

                 _____

                 2. Man to Man Marking or Zonal System

                 _____

                 Side Team Funnels to_____

                 Types of Pressure and When They Are Used _____

                 _____

                 Offsides Trap_____

How Team Defends: Corners _____

                      Free Kicks _____

                      Penalty Kicks _____

                      Kick-Offs _____

Overall Team Strengths _____

Overall Team Weaknesses _____

Keys to Victory   1. _____

                 2. _____

                 3. _____

Player Comments_____

_____

TM

Game 2

Joe Bertuzzi's
Soccer Scounting Guide

_____Scout Guide

TEAM NAME

For The Season of 20____

vs

_____   _____

Away Opponent   **Home Opponent**

_____   _____

Field Size   **Conditions of the Field**

_____   _____

Kickoff Time   **Weather Conditions**

_____   _____

Halftime Score   **Final Score**

_____   _____

Date: **Prepared By:**

Goalkeeper Pregame Assessment

_____GK is/is not in set position prior to shot

———GK does/does not take attacking step

———GK does/does not properly cut down angle

Collapse Dive Technique

_____

_____

Extension Dive Technique

_____

_____

Handling of Crosses

_____

_____

Parrying Balls

_____

_____

Boxing Balls

_____

_____

Tipping Balls

_____

_____

Breakaway Saves

_____

_____

Distribution

_____

_____

GK Strengths

_____

_____

GK Weaknesses

_____

_____

Team System of Play

System of Play

Key Players within the System

Weak Links within the System

System of Play - Players within the System

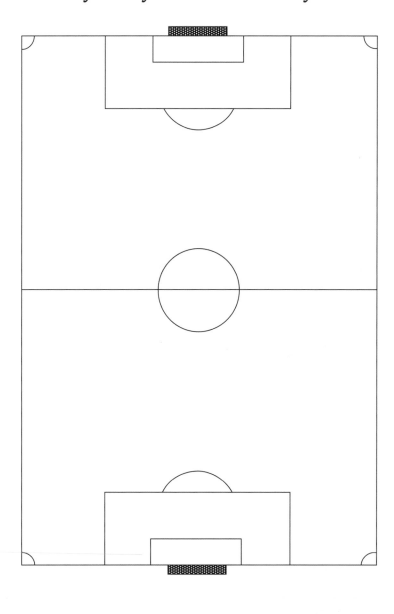

Individual Player Assessments

Players who need Special Attention

_____

Weak Link Players

_____

Coaches Notes:

_____

_____

_____

_____

_____

_____

_____

_____

_____

_____

_____

PA

Game 3

Goalkeeper   #   Jersey Color   Name

Technical/Tactical Observations:

Strengths:

Weaknesses:

Position   #   Name   Left/Right Foot

Technical/Tactical Observations:

Strengths:

Weaknesses:

Position   #   Name   Left/Right Foot

Technical/Tactical Observations:

Strengths:

Weaknesses:

Position   #   Name   Left/Right Foot

Technical/Tactical Observations:

Strengths:

Weaknesses:

Position   #   Name   Left/Right Foot

Technical/Tactical Observations:

Strengths:

Weaknesses:

Individual Player Assessments

Starting Team

Position   #   Name   Left/Right Foot _____
Technical/Tactical Observations:

Strengths: _____
Weaknesses:

Position   #   Name   Left/Right Foot _____
Technical/Tactical Observations:

Strengths: _____
Weaknesses:

Position   #   Name   Left/Right Foot _____
Technical/Tactical Observations:

Strengths: _____
Weaknesses:

Position   #   Name   Left/Right Foot _____
Technical/Tactical Observations:

Strengths: _____
Weaknesses:

Position   #   Name   Left/Right Foot _____
Technical/Tactical Observations:

Strengths: _____
Weaknesses:

Position   #   Name   Left/Right Foot _____
Technical/Tactical Observations:

Strengths: _____
Weaknesses:

Individual Player Assessments

Position   #   Name   Left/Right Foot
Technical/Tactical Observations:

Strengths:
Weaknesses:

Position   #   Name   Left/Right Foot
Technical/Tactical Observations:

Strengths:
Weaknesses:

Position   #   Name   Left/Right Foot
Technical/Tactical Observations:

Strengths:
Weaknesses:

Position   #   Name   Left/Right Foot
Technical/Tactical Observations:

Strengths:
Weaknesses:

Position   #   Name   Left/Right Foot
Technical/Tactical Observations:

Strengths:
Weaknesses:

Position   #   Name   Left/Right Foot
Technical/Tactical Observations:

Strengths:
Weaknesses:

Key to Diagrams

X = Attacker

O = Defender

- - - - - - → = Movement of Ball

———————→ = Movement of Player

∿∿∿→ = Movement of Player Dribbling the Ball

⌒→ = Curved Shot or Service

(22) = Circled number is the location a player has scored from

10. = A dot next to a number is where the ball is located prior to a set piece

The Attack

_____ Direct Style of Play

_____ Indirect Style of Play

_____Direct Forward Without Intent

Key Players to Mark on Corners

_____

Key Players to Mark on Free Kicks

_____

Key Players Over the Ball on Free Kicks

_____

Players(s) with a Long Throw-in_____

Coaches Notes:

_____

_____

_____

_____

_____

_____

_____

_____

_____

The Attack - Tactics

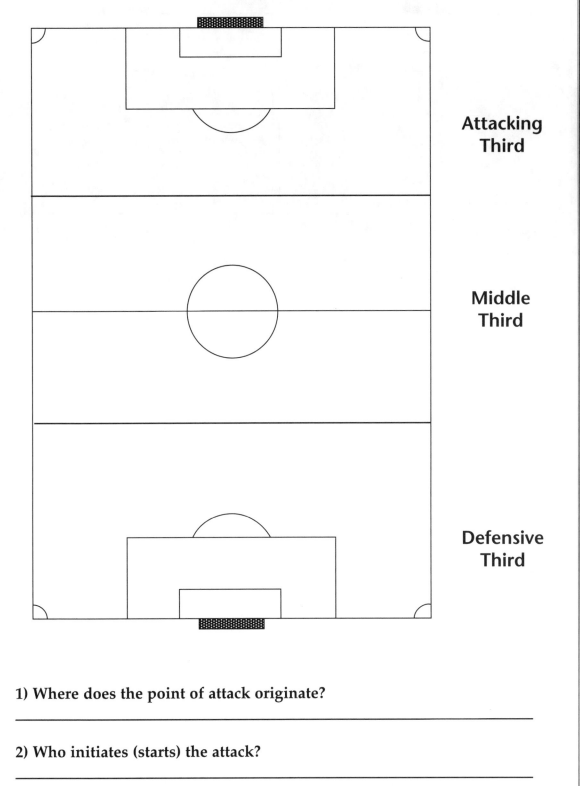

Attacking
Third

Middle
Third

Defensive
Third

1) Where does the point of attack originate?

_____

2) Who initiates (starts) the attack?

_____

3) Who does the playmaker primarily get the ball from?

_____

The Attack - Corner Kicks

AC

Game 3

Coaches Notes:

_____

_____

_____

_____

_____

_____

_____

_____

_____

_____

The Attack - Free Kicks

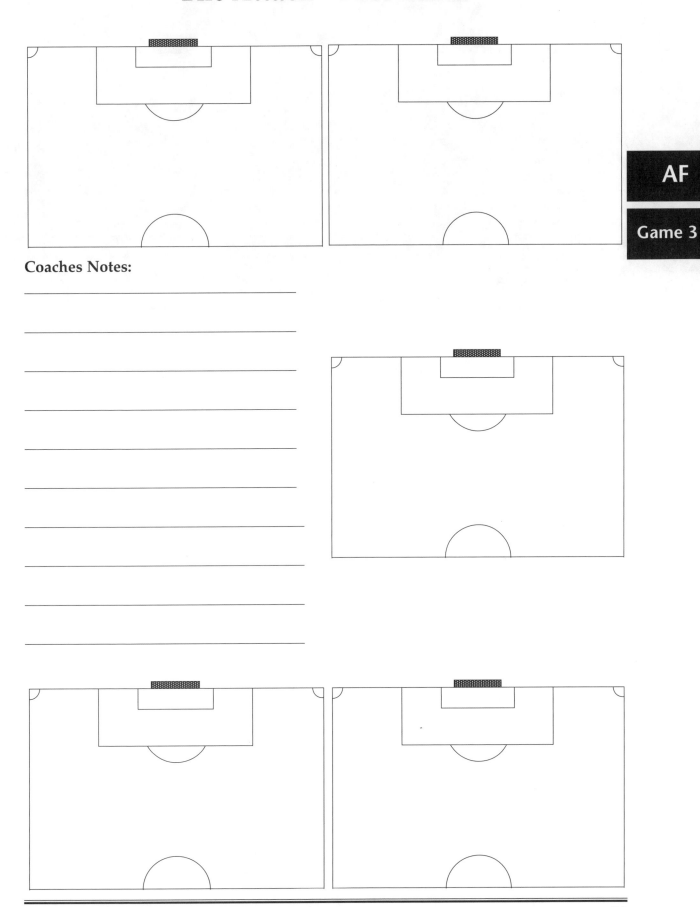

Coaches Notes:

_____

_____

_____

_____

_____

_____

_____

_____

_____

The Attack - Throw-ins

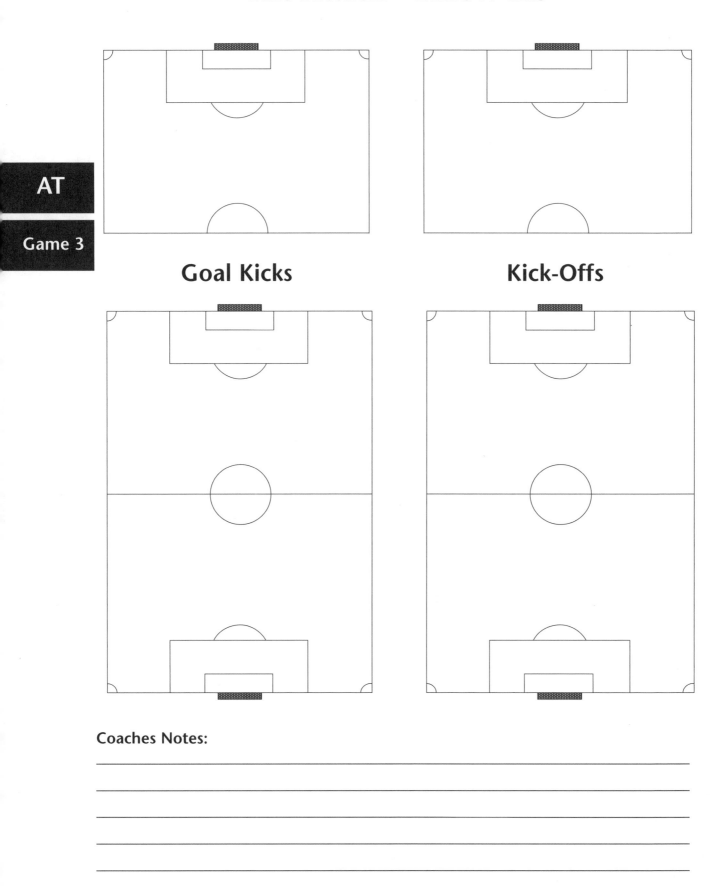

Goal Kicks

Kick-Offs

Coaches Notes:

_____

_____

_____

_____

_____

The Attack - Scoring Opportunities

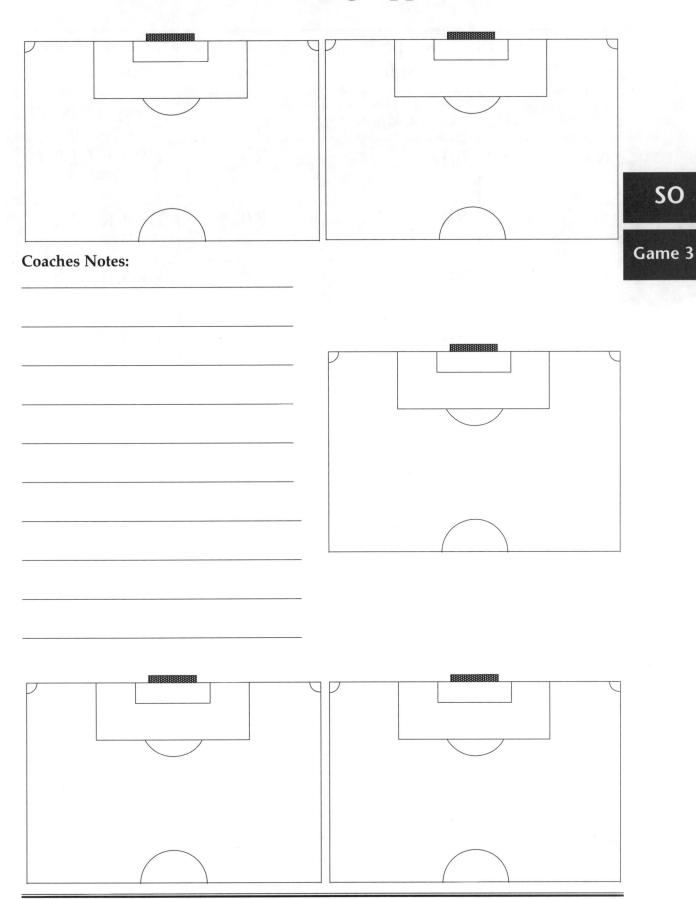

Coaches Notes:

_____

_____

_____

_____

_____

_____

_____

_____

_____

Penalty Kicks

Shooter	Keeper's Side	Shooter's Foot	Corner Shot was taken to
	Shot Was Taken To		(Keeper's Side)
#	R/L	R/L	UR/LR UL/LL
#	R/L	R/L	UR/LR UL/LL
#	R/L	R/L	UR/LR UL/LL
#	R/L	R/L	UR/LR UL/LL
#	R/L	R/L	UR/LR UL/LL

Key To Penalty Kicks
R = Right
L = Left
UR = Upper Right
LR = Lower Right
UL = Upper Left
LL = Lower Left

Coaches Notes:_____
_____
_____
_____
_____
_____
_____
_____

Goalkeeper Defending PK:

Range to Post_____

Better Diving Side_____

Does he Read the Shooter or Pick A Side_____

Is he Poised Prior to the Shot_____

The Defense

_____Sweeper Stopper System

_____Flat Back System (3 Defenders/4 Defenders)

_____Man to Man Marking System

_____Zonal Defense Marking System

_____Side Team Funnels To_____

_____High Pressure - What Times During Match

_____

_____

_____

_____Low Pressure - What Times During Match

_____

_____

_____

_____Offsides Trap - Where and When

_____

_____

_____

The Defense - Tactics

DT

Game 3

Attacking
Third

Middle
Third

Defensive
Third

1) Where do they draw their line of defense?
_____

2) Regardless of the system of play, do they track well?
_____

3) How well do they pressure the ball and how many numbers do they get
in behind the ball?_____

The Defense - Corner Kicks

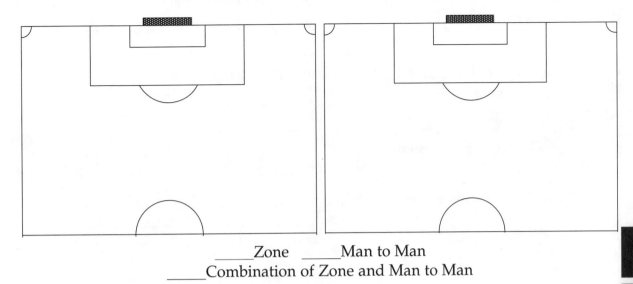

_____Zone _____Man to Man
_____Combination of Zone and Man to Man

Free Kicks

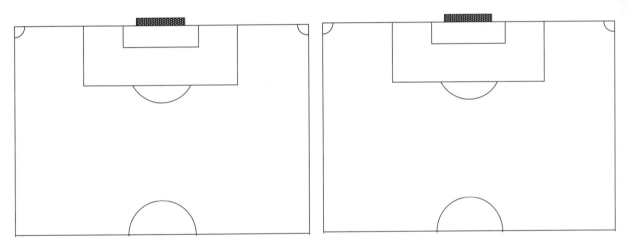

1. #_____Sets the Wall   2. Organized/Not Organized in Setting Wall
3. Fast/Slow in Setting Wall   4. Pressured/No Pressure on Ball

Penalty Kicks

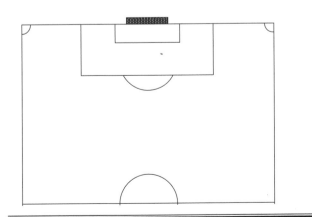

Kick Offs

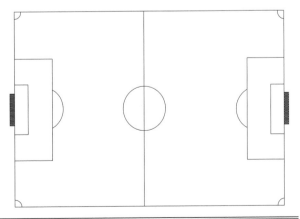

Team Meeting Prep Sheet

Date of Game_____Game Time_____Location _____

Opponent_____Size of Field _____

<u>**Summary of Opponents Strengths and Weaknesses**</u>

System of Play_____

Style of Play_____

Key Players within System   Attack:_____

Defense:_____

Weak Links within System   Attack:_____

Defense:_____

Goalkeeping _____

Key Players to Mark on Corners _____

Key Players to Mark on Free Kicks _____

Player(s) with a Long Throw-in _____

Penalty Kick Shooter _____

Defending   1. Sweeper Stopper or Flat Back System 3/4

_____

2. Man to Man Marking or Zonal System

_____

Side Team Funnels to_____

Types of Pressure and When They Are Used _____

_____

Offsides Trap_____

How Team Defends: Corners _____

Free Kicks _____

Penalty Kicks _____

Kick-Offs _____

Overall Team Strengths _____

Overall Team Weaknesses _____

Keys to Victory   1. _____

2. _____

3. _____

Player Comments_____

_____

Joe Bertuzzi's
Soccer Scounting Guide

_____Scout Guide

TEAM NAME

For The Season of 20____

vs

_____   _____

Away Opponent   **Home Opponent**

_____   _____

Field Size   **Conditions of the Field**

_____   _____

Kickoff Time   **Weather Conditions**

_____   _____

Halftime Score   **Final Score**

_____   _____

Date: **Prepared By:**

Goalkeeper Pregame Assessment

_____GK is/is not in set position prior to shot

———GK does/does not take attacking step

———GK does/does not properly cut down angle

Collapse Dive Technique
_____
_____

Extension Dive Technique
_____
_____

Handling of Crosses
_____
_____

Parrying Balls
_____
_____

Boxing Balls
_____
_____

Tipping Balls
_____
_____

Breakaway Saves
_____
_____

Distribution
_____
_____

GK Strengths
_____
_____

GK Weaknesses
_____
_____

Team System of Play

SP

Game 4

System of Play

Key Players within the System

Weak Links within the System

System of Play - Players within the System

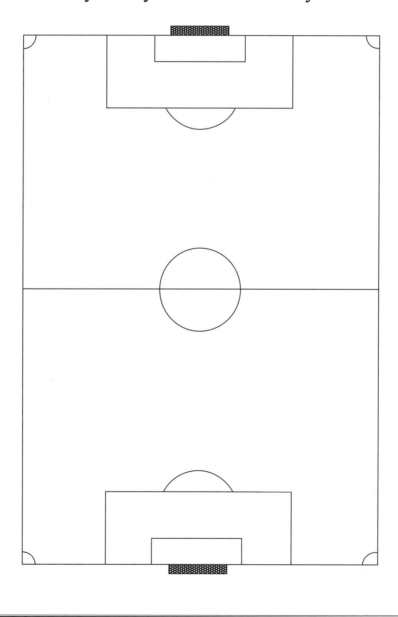

Individual Player Assessments

Players who need Special Attention

_____

Weak Link Players

_____

Coaches Notes:

_____

_____

_____

_____

_____

_____

_____

_____

_____

_____

PA

Game 4

Goalkeeper   #   Jersey Color   Name

Technical/Tactical Observations:

Strengths:

Weaknesses:

Position   #   Name   Left/Right Foot

Technical/Tactical Observations:

Strengths:

Weaknesses:

Position   #   Name   Left/Right Foot

Technical/Tactical Observations:

Strengths:

Weaknesses:

Position   #   Name   Left/Right Foot

Technical/Tactical Observations:

Strengths:

Weaknesses:

Position   #   Name   Left/Right Foot

Technical/Tactical Observations:

Strengths:

Weaknesses:

Individual Player Assessments

Starting Team

Position   #   Name   Left/Right Foot
Technical/Tactical Observations:

Strengths:
Weaknesses:

Position   #   Name   Left/Right Foot
Technical/Tactical Observations:

Strengths:
Weaknesses:

Position   #   Name   Left/Right Foot
Technical/Tactical Observations:

Strengths:
Weaknesses:

Position   #   Name   Left/Right Foot
Technical/Tactical Observations:

Strengths:
Weaknesses:

Position   #   Name   Left/Right Foot
Technical/Tactical Observations:

Strengths:
Weaknesses:

Position   #   Name   Left/Right Foot
Technical/Tactical Observations:

Strengths:
Weaknesses:

PA

Game 4

Position   #   Name   Left/Right Foot
Technical/Tactical Observations:

Strengths:
Weaknesses:

Position   #   Name   Left/Right Foot
Technical/Tactical Observations:

Strengths:
Weaknesses:

Position   #   Name   Left/Right Foot
Technical/Tactical Observations:

Strengths:
Weaknesses:

Position   #   Name   Left/Right Foot
Technical/Tactical Observations:

Strengths:
Weaknesses:

Position   #   Name   Left/Right Foot
Technical/Tactical Observations:

Strengths:
Weaknesses:

Position   #   Name   Left/Right Foot
Technical/Tactical Observations:

Strengths:
Weaknesses:

Key to Diagrams

X = Attacker

O = Defender

 ---------► = Movement of Ball

─────────► = Movement of Player

∿∿∿∿► = Movement of Player Dribbling the Ball

⌒► = Curved Shot or Service

(22) = Circled number is the location a player has scored from

10. = A dot next to a number is where the ball is located prior to a set piece

The Attack

_____Direct Style of Play

_____Indirect Style of Play

_____Direct Forward Without Intent

Key Players to Mark on Corners

_____

Key Players to Mark on Free Kicks

_____

Key Players Over the Ball on Free Kicks

_____

Players(s) with a Long Throw-in_____

Coaches Notes:

_____

_____

_____

_____

_____

_____

_____

_____

The Attack - Tactics

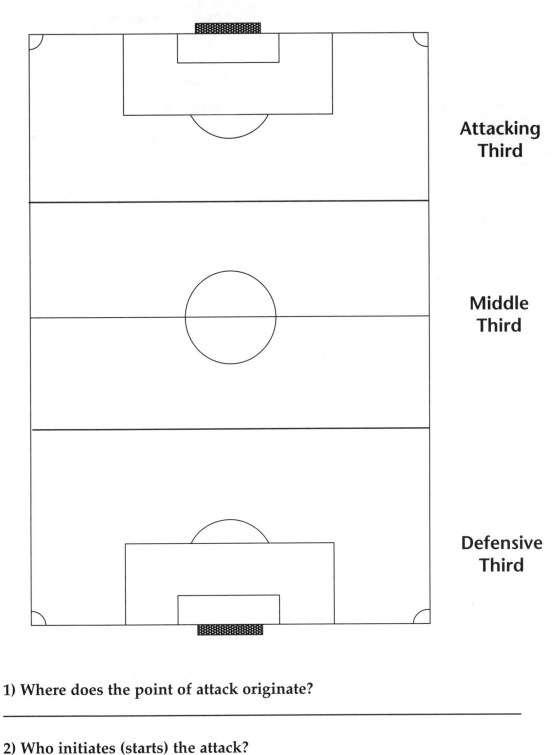

Attacking Third

Middle Third

Defensive Third

1) Where does the point of attack originate?

_____

2) Who initiates (starts) the attack?

_____

3) Who does the playmaker primarily get the ball from?

_____

The Attack - Corner Kicks

Coaches Notes:

_____

_____

_____

_____

_____

_____

_____

_____

_____

The Attack - Free Kicks

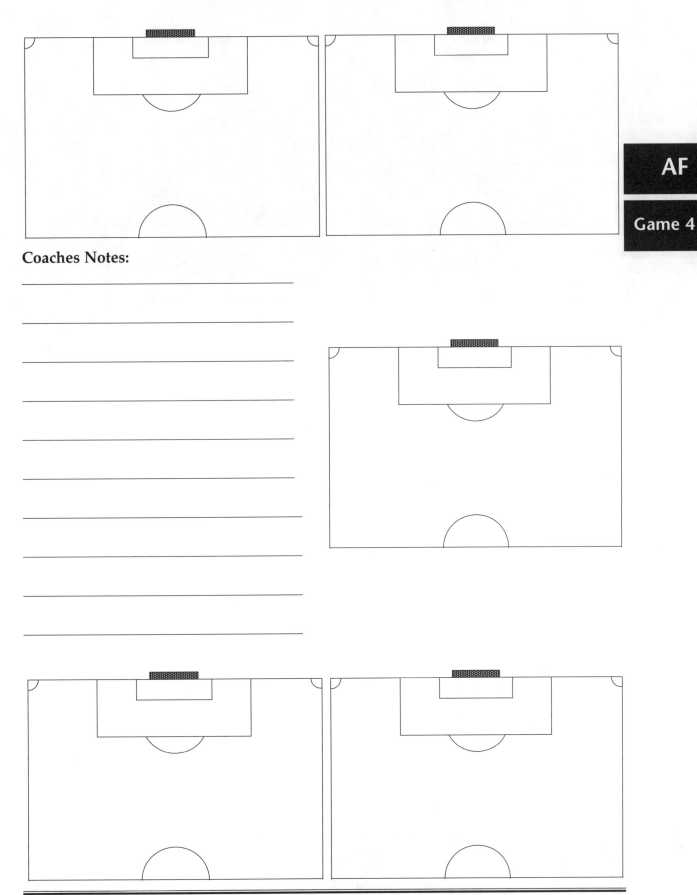

Coaches Notes:

_____

_____

_____

_____

_____

_____

_____

_____

_____

_____

_____

The Attack - Throw-ins

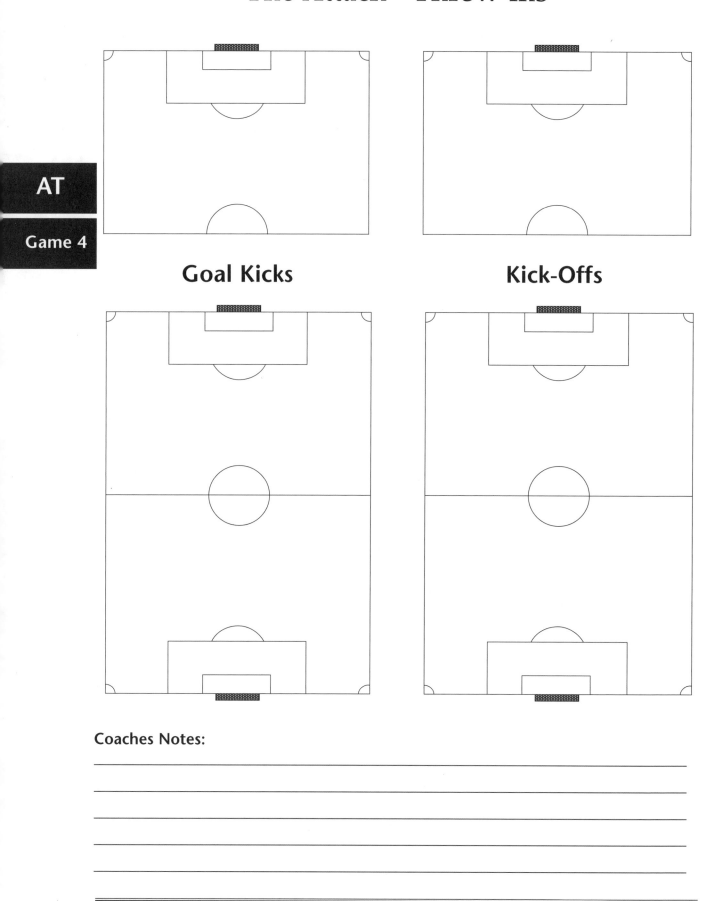

Goal Kicks

Kick-Offs

Coaches Notes:

_____

_____

_____

_____

_____

The Attack - Scoring Opportunities

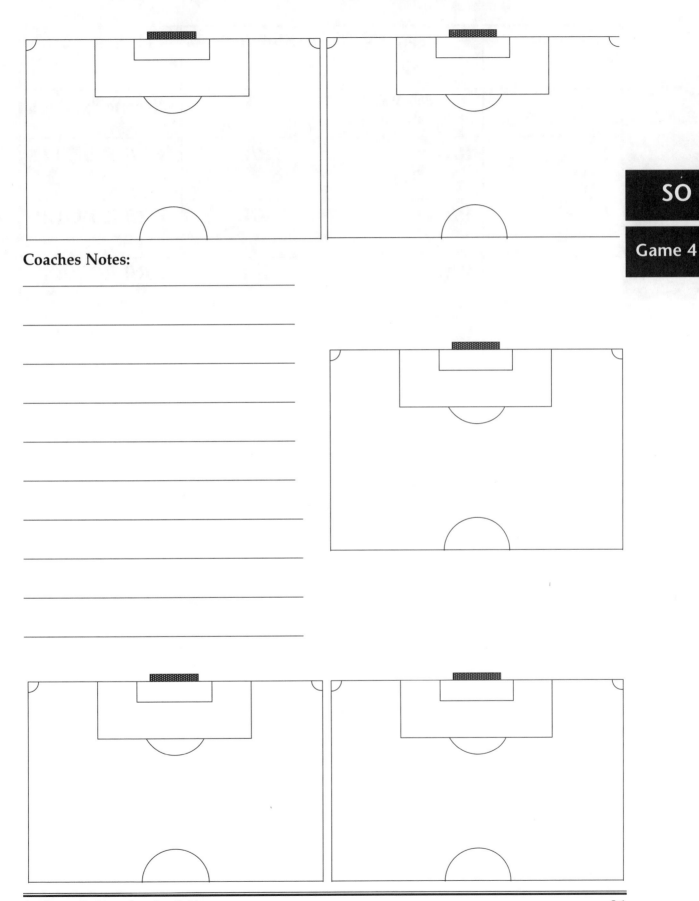

Coaches Notes:

Penalty Kicks

Shooter	Keeper's Side	Shooter's Foot	Corner Shot was taken to
	Shot Was Taken To		(Keeper's Side)
#	R/L	R/L	UR/LR UL/LL
#	R/L	R/L	UR/LR UL/LL
#	R/L	R/L	UR/LR UL/LL
#	R/L	R/L	UR/LR UL/LL
#	R/L	R/L	UR/LR UL/LL

Key To Penalty Kicks
R = Right
L = Left
UR = Upper Right
LR = Lower Right
UL = Upper Left
LL = Lower Left

Coaches Notes:_____
_____
_____
_____
_____
_____
_____
_____

Goalkeeper Defending PK:

Range to Post_____

Better Diving Side_____

Does he Read the Shooter or Pick A Side_____

Is he Poised Prior to the Shot_____

The Defense

_____Sweeper Stopper System

_____Flat Back System (3 Defenders/4 Defenders)

_____Man to Man Marking System

_____Zonal Defense Marking System

_____Side Team Funnels To_____

_____High Pressure - What Times During Match

_____
_____
_____

_____Low Pressure - What Times During Match

_____
_____
_____

_____Offsides Trap - Where and When

_____
_____
_____

The Defense - Tactics

Attacking
Third

Middle
Third

Defensive
Third

1) Where do they draw their line of defense?

_____

2) Regardless of the system of play, do they track well?

_____

3) How well do they pressure the ball and how many numbers do they get
in behind the ball?_____

The Defense - Corner Kicks

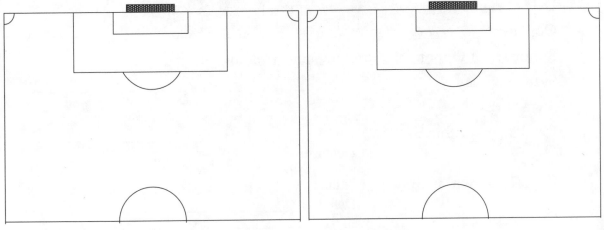

_____Zone _____Man to Man
_____Combination of Zone and Man to Man

Free Kicks

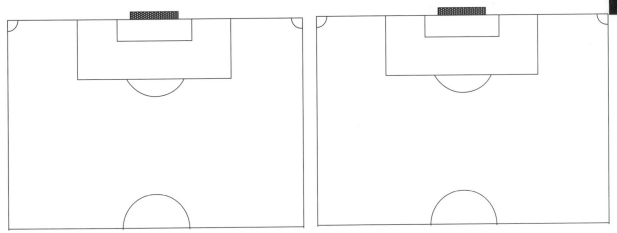

1. #_____Sets the Wall   2. Organized/Not Organized in Setting Wall
3. Fast/Slow in Setting Wall   4. Pressured/No Pressure on Ball

Penalty Kicks

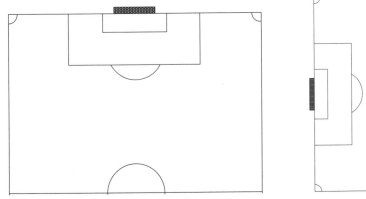

Kick Offs

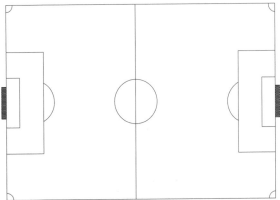

Team Meeting Prep Sheet

Date of Game_____Game Time_____Location _____

Opponent_____Size of Field _____

Summary of Opponents Strengths and Weaknesses

System of Play_____

Style of Play_____

Key Players within System   Attack:_____

                        Defense:_____

Weak Links within System   Attack:_____

                        Defense:_____

Goalkeeping _____

Key Players to Mark on Corners _____

Key Players to Mark on Free Kicks _____

Player(s) with a Long Throw-in _____

Penalty Kick Shooter _____

Defending   1. Sweeper Stopper or Flat Back System 3/4

          _____

          2. Man to Man Marking or Zonal System

          _____

          Side Team Funnels to_____

          Types of Pressure and When They Are Used _____

          _____

          Offsides Trap_____

How Team Defends: Corners _____

                   Free Kicks _____

                   Penalty Kicks _____

                   Kick-Offs _____

Overall Team Strengths _____

Overall Team Weaknesses _____

Keys to Victory   1. _____

              2. _____

              3. _____

Player Comments_____

_____